THE MESSAGE
OF JESUS:
LEADER GUIDE

THE MESSAGE OF JESUS
WORDS THAT CHANGED THE WORLD

978-1-7910-3421-4 *Paperback*
978-1-7910-3422-1 *eBook*
978-1-7910-3426-9 *Large Print*

DVD
978-1-7910-3425-2

Leader Guide
978-1-7910-3423-8
978-1-7910-3424-5 *eBook*

Also by Adam Hamilton

24 Hours That Changed the World

Christianity and World Religions

Christianity's Family Tree

Confronting the Controversies

Creed

Enough

Faithful

Final Words from the Cross

Forgiveness

Half Truths

Incarnation

John

Leading Beyond the Walls

Living Unafraid

Love to Stay

Luke

Making Sense of the Bible

Moses

Not a Silent Night

Prepare the Way for the Lord

Revival

Seeing Gray in a World of Black and White

Simon Peter

Speaking Well

The Call

The Journey

The Lord's Prayer

The Walk

The Way

Unafraid

When Christians Get It Wrong

Wrestling with Doubt, Finding Faith

Words of Life

Why?

For more information, visit AdamHamilton.com.

ADAM HAMILTON

Author of *John, The Walk,* and *24 Hours That Changed the World*

THE MESSAGE OF JESUS

WORDS THAT CHANGED THE WORLD

LEADER GUIDE

Abingdon Press | Nashville

THE MESSAGE OF JESUS
WORDS THAT CHANGED THE WORLD
LEADER GUIDE

Copyright © 2024 Abingdon Press
All rights reserved.

978-1-7910-3423-8

Scripture quotations unless noted otherwise are taken from the New Revised Standard Version, Updated Edition. Copyright © 2021 National Council of Churches of Christ in the United States of America. Used by permission. All rights reserved worldwide.

Scripture quotation noted CEB is taken from the Common English Bible, copyright 2011. Used by permission. All rights reserved.

MANUFACTURED IN THE UNITED STATES OF AMERICA

CONTENTS

ABOUT THE LEADER GUIDE WRITER

The Rev. Michael S. Poteet is an ordained Minister of Word and Sacrament in the Presbyterian Church (U.S.A.). A graduate of the College of William and Mary and Princeton Theological Seminary, he serves the larger church as a Christian education writer, biblical storyteller, and guest preacher. You can find his occasional musings on the meetings of faith and fiction at http://www.bibliomike.com.

INTRODUCTION

In *The Message of Jesus*, Adam Hamilton invites readers to consider how the words *of* Jesus, rather than simply words *about* Jesus, inform and shape their understanding and living of the Christian faith. From Jesus's initial "sermon" about the coming kingdom of God to the questions Jesus asked and the commissions he gave after his resurrection, Adam acquaints readers again, or perhaps for the first time, with Jesus's words as recorded in the Gospels, challenging us all to let them mold us into more faithful disciples.

This Leader Guide is intended to help you lead a small group of adults from your congregation in such an encounter with Jesus through Bible study. It gives you logistical pointers, Scripture readings, and study questions you can use to plan and lead six sessions, corresponding to the six chapters of *The Message of Jesus*:

- **Session 1: The Kingdom of God Has Come Near.** Jesus's first public message was brief and blunt. How does his urgent announcement of God's reign matter to us and to the world, two thousand years later?
- **Session 2: The World's Most Important Sermon.** The "Sermon on the Mount" is, at one and the same time, among the most familiar passages of Scripture and the most challenging. How does this collection of Jesus's teachings continue to provoke a vision of life in Jesus's community?
- **Session 3: Jesus Spoke to Them in Parables.** A masterful storyteller, Jesus used brief fictional narratives to communicate

God's truth. How do some of his most familiar parables challenge preconceptions about being Christian today?

- **Session 4: Who Do YOU Say That I Am?** Jesus asks his followers, then and now, to confess their convictions about who he is and what he means. How do Jesus's words about himself in the Gospel of John help us answer his questions today?
- **Session 5: Final Words.** At his last supper with his disciples and from his cross, Jesus spoke words that have echoed through the church and world for two millennia. How does what Jesus said before his death shape our lives as his followers now?
- **Session 6: The Resurrection and the Life.** Jesus taught about heaven and the next life. What makes his messages on this subject relevant to life today and in the world to come?

Although this Leader Guide is written with the assumption that both leaders and participants will also be reading *The Message of Jesus*, its quotations from Adam's book and its direct quotations of and references to Scripture mean it can also be used on its own.

Each session contains the following elements to draw from as you plan six in-person, virtual, or hybrid sessions:

- Session Goals
- Biblical Foundations–List of scripture texts for the session.
- Before Your Session–Tips to help you prepare a productive session.
- Starting Your Session–Discussion questions intended to "warm up" your group for fruitful discussion.
- Watch Session Video
- Opening Prayer
- Book Discussion Questions–You likely will not be able or want to use all the questions in every session, so feel free to pick and choose based on your group's interests and the Spirit's leading.
- Closing Your Session–A focused discussion or reflection, often suggesting action to take beyond the session.

- Closing Prayer
- Optional Extensions–Ideas for further discussion and other activities to enhance your study.

Helpful Tips for Preparing, Leading, and Adapting Your Study Sessions

Below are a few helpful tips for preparing and leading your study sessions, each week, as well as for adapting your sessions to online meetings if desired.

Preparation

- Pray for the leading of the Holy Spirit as you prepare for the study. Pray for discernment for yourself and for each member of the study group.
- Before each session, familiarize yourself with the content. Read the book chapter again and watch the video segment. Read the Scripture passages that support each lesson. Feel free to consult different translations.
- Read through the lesson plan, then go back and choose the activities and questions you wish to use during the session. Plan carefully, yet also be prepared to adjust the session as group members interact and questions arise. Allow space for the Holy Spirit to move in and through the material, the group members, and you as facilitator.
- Secure in advance a TV and DVD player or a computer with projection.
- Prepare the space so that it will enhance the learning process. Ideally, group members should be seated around a table or in a circle so that all can see each other. Movable chairs are best so participants may easily form pairs or small groups for discussion.
- Bring a supply of Bibles for those who forget to bring their own. Having a variety of translations is helpful.

- For each session you will also need a whiteboard and markers, a chalkboard and chalk, or an easel with paper and markers.

Leading

- Begin and end on time.
- Create a climate of openness, encouraging group members to participate as they feel comfortable. Remember that some people will jump right in with answers and comments, while others will need time to process what is being discussed.
- If you notice that some group members don't enter the conversation, ask them if they have thoughts to share. Give everyone a chance to talk, but keep the conversation moving. Try to prevent a few individuals from doing all the talking.
- Communicate the importance of group discussions and group activities.
- If no one answers at first during discussions, don't be afraid of pauses. Count silently to ten; then say something such as "Would anyone like to go first?" If no one responds, venture an answer yourself and ask for comments.
- Model openness as you share with the group. Group members will follow your example. If you limit your sharing to a surface level, others will follow suit.
- Encourage multiple answers or responses before moving on.
- Ask, "Why?" or "Why do you believe that?" or "Can you say more about that?" to help continue a discussion and give it greater depth.
- Affirm others' responses with comments such as "Great" or "Thanks" or "Good insight."
- Monitor your own contributions. If you find yourself doing most of the talking, back off so that you don't train the group to listen rather than speak up.
- Remember that you don't have all the answers. Your job is to keep the discussion going and encourage participation.

- Involve group members in various aspects of the group session, such as playing the videos, saying prayers, or reading Scripture.
- Note that the session plans sometimes call for breaking into smaller groups. This gives everyone a chance to speak and participate fully. Mix up the teams; don't let the same people pair up on every activity.
- Because many activities call for personal sharing, confidentiality is essential. Group members should never pass along stories that have been shared in the group. Remind the group members at each session: confidentiality is crucial to the success of this study.

Adapting for Online Meetings

Meeting online is a great option for a number of situations. When circumstances preclude meeting in person, online meetings are a welcome opportunity for people to converse while seeing each other's faces. Online meetings can also expand the "neighborhood" of possible group members, because people can log in from just about anywhere in the world. This also gives those who do not have access to transportation or who prefer not to travel at certain times of day the chance to participate.

One popular option is Zoom. This platform is used quite a bit by businesses. If your church has an account, this can be a good medium. Google Meet, Webex, and Microsoft Teams are other good choices. Individuals can obtain free accounts for each of these platforms, but there may be restrictions (for instance, Zoom's free version limits meetings to forty minutes). Check each platform's website to be sure you are aware of any such restrictions before you sign up.

Video Sharing
- All of the videoconferencing platforms mentioned above support screen-sharing videos. Some have specific requirements for assuring that sound will play clearly in addition to the videos. Follow your videoconferencing platform instructions carefully, and test the video sharing in advance to be sure it works.

- If you wish to screen-share a DVD video, you may need to use a different media player. Some media players will not allow you to share your screen when you play copyright-protected DVDs. VLC is a free media player that is safe and easy to use. To try this software, download at videolan.org/VLC.
- *What about copyright?* DVDs like those you use for group study are meant to be used in a group setting "real time." That is, whether you meet in person, online, or in a hybrid setting, Abingdon Press encourages use of your DVD or streaming video.
- *What is allowed?* Streaming an Abingdon DVD over Zoom, Teams, or similar platform during a small-group session.
- *What is not allowed?* Posting video of a published DVD study to social media or YouTube for later viewing.
- If you have any questions about permissions and copyright, email permissions@abingdonpress.com.
- The streaming subscription platform Amplify Media makes it easy to share streaming videos for groups. When your church has an Amplify subscription, your group members can sign on and have access to the video sessions.
- Visit AmplifyMedia.com to learn more.

Training and Practice
- Choose a platform and practice using it, so you are comfortable with it. Engage in a couple of practice runs with another person.
- Set up a training meeting.
- In advance, teach participants how to log in. Tell them that you will send them an invitation via email, and that it will include a link for them to click at the time of the meeting.
- For those who do not have internet service, let them know they may telephone into the meeting. Provide them the number and let them know that there is usually a unique phone number for each meeting.

- During the training meeting, show them the basic tools available for them to use. They can learn other tools as they feel more confident.

During the Meetings
- *Early invitations.* Send out invitations at least a week in advance. Many meeting platforms enable you to do this through their software.
- *Early log in.* Participants should log in at least ten minutes in advance to test their audio and their video connections.
- *Talking/not talking.* Instruct participants to keep their microphones muted during the meeting, so extraneous noise from their location does not interrupt the meeting. This includes chewing or yawning sounds, which can be embarrassing! When it is time for discussion, participants can unmute themselves. However, ask them to raise their hand or wave when they are ready to share, so you can call on them. Give folks a few minutes to speak up. They may not be used to conversing in web conferences.

Thank you for your willingness to lead. May you and your group experience a fresh and powerful encounter with the message of Jesus!

SESSION 1

THE KINGDOM OF GOD
HAS COME NEAR

Session Goals

This session's reading, reflection, discussion, and prayer will help participants:

- Think about the way quotations can "sum up" famous people and important people in their own lives, and about how frequently or infrequently Christians today quote Jesus to summarize their faith.
- Reflect on the biblical image of God as king and its meaning in modern society.
- Examine Jesus's first sermon in Mark 1:14–15 for information about what the "kingdom of God" meant to him, and what it can mean for Christians today.
- Explore Jesus's parables of the mustard seed and the yeast from Matthew 13.
- Articulate the tension between the "already" and "not yet" nature of God's kingdom, and identify ways they can participate in "closing the gap" between the two.

Biblical Foundations

- Psalm 99:1-4
- Mark 1:14-15
- Matthew 13:31-33

Before Your Session

- Carefully and prayerfully read this session's Biblical Foundations, more than once. Note words and phrases that attract your attention and meditate on them. Write down questions you have and try to answer them, consulting trusted Bible commentaries.
- Carefully read the introduction and chapter 1 of *The Message of Jesus*, more than once.
- You will need: Bibles for in-person participants and/or screen slides prepared with scripture texts for sharing (identify the translation used); newsprint or a markerboard and markers (for in-person sessions); paper, pens or pencils (in-person).
- If using the DVD or streaming video, preview the session 1 video segment. Choose the best time in your session plan for viewing it.
- If necessary, prepare handouts and/or a slide for screen sharing with a translation of Psalm 99:1-4 that all participants can read together.

Starting Your Session

Welcome participants. Tell them why you are excited to study *The Message of Jesus* by Adam Hamilton with them. Invite them to speak briefly about why they are interested in this study and what they hope to gain from it.

Lead your group in brainstorming a list of familiar quotations from famous people, past and/or present. (For purposes of this introductory activity, leave Jesus off the list.) Especially encourage participants to offer quotations they think "sum up" a person's life or teachings, and ask them to explain why. Write key words from these quotations on newsprint or markerboard.

Invite participants to offer quotations "famous" in their own lives for "summing up" the life or outlook of someone they know, respect, or love *(for example, "My grandmother always said…"* or *"My favorite teacher liked to say…").*

Summarize Adam's observation from the introduction that "when Christians today summarize their faith, they often do so by speaking of Jesus's death for their sins and his resurrection," but don't often directly quote his words. Discuss:

- Does Adam's observation surprise you? Do you agree with it? Why or why not?
- Why do you think the apostle Paul, arguably the most influential early interpreter of Jesus's message, only directly quotes Jesus once? Why does he quote Jesus in 1 Corinthians 11:23-25?
- Why do you think the church's historic creeds, such as the Apostles' Creed, don't quote Jesus?
- When you summarize your faith, or if you were asked to do so now, do or would you quote Jesus's words? If yes, which ones? If not, why not?
- Why does Adam say it's important for Jesus's followers today to know Jesus's words?
- Think about sayings of and words from Jesus that you know. Would you "nominate" any of them as "most important"? If so, which one(s)? If not, why not?

Tell participants that during this study, your group will read and reflect on some of Jesus's most important words, as recorded in the four New Testament Gospels. This session highlights words at the heart of Jesus's message, words about the kingdom of God.

Opening Prayer

Blessed are you, Lord God, ruler of the universe—sovereign over all creation, over all the nations, and over every human heart. As we begin this season of study together, may your Holy Spirit lead us to willingly submit our hearts to your loving rule, that we may acclaim you as our rightful king and live as your increasingly faithful subjects, to the glory of him whose message we long to hear again, your Son Jesus Christ. Amen.

Watch Session Video

Watch the session 1 video segment together. Discuss:

- Which of Adam's statements most interested, intrigued, surprised, or confused you? Why?
- What questions does this video segment raise for you?

Keep the video session in mind throughout your discussion of the book and Bible below.

Book Discussion Questions

A Foundational Assertion: God Is King

Read Psalm 99:1-4 in unison (using the handout and/or slide you prepared before your session). Discuss:

- Why do these verses praise God as a king? What responses do these verses present as appropriate to God the king?
- How is God's kingship, as described in these verses, like and/ or unlike human kingship?
- Adam writes, "The Old Testament repeatedly affirms that God rules as king of the heavens, king of creation, king of the earth, and king of Israel." What other Old Testament passages can you recall or find that present God as king in each of these ways?

- What distinction, if any, do you see between recognizing God as the universal sovereign and recognizing God as one's personal sovereign? Are these affirmations equally important? Why or why not?
- How easily or comfortably do you use this biblical image for God, and why?
- Do other images convey what Adam calls the "foundational assertion" that "God is the rightful king or ruler over creation?" If so, which ones? If none do, why not?
- How would you respond to someone who is uncomfortable thinking of or addressing God as king?

The Revolution Jesus Launched

Recruit a volunteer to read aloud Mark 1:14-15. Discuss:

- What can we learn about God as king from Jesus's "first recorded sermon" in Mark?
- How do you understand "the kingdom of God" (or "reign of God")? What about this Kingdom is good news?
- Why are repentance and belief the responses to the Kingdom for which Jesus calls?
- Adam explains that humanity's need to repent is as old as the garden of Eden. How did Adam and Eve rebel against God's kingship? What makes their story, as Adam calls it, "the archetypal story of humanity"?
- Adam names several situations in which he sees idolatry as a temptation today. Where do you see "societies and nations" struggling (or perhaps failing to struggle) with idolatry? How do you struggle with idolatry in your own life? How does your congregation struggle with idolatry?
- What was, and continues to be, the nature of the "revolution" Jesus launched, according to Adam? What was, and is, this revolution's goal? How did it differ from the revolution some people in first-century Judea expected or wanted—and from the revolutions for which some people look today?

- Adam shares what he said to his Jewish tour guide in Israel who "knew so much about Jesus and...truly loved him...[but did] not believe that Jesus was the Messiah." Adam doesn't tell us how, if at all, his tour guide responded. What do you think of the tour guide's objections? What do you think of Adam's response? How would you have responded?
- Jesus's followers "were and are revolutionaries," writes Adam, "who loved their neighbors, and even their enemies." Who are some specific Christians you know or know of who seek or have sought "to live as those who longed to see the kingdom of God come on earth as it is in heaven"?
- Adam says one sin of which individual Christians and the church must repent is "hav[ing] often failed to live as those who are part of, and [who are] ushering in, the kingdom of God." What does such repentance look like, in practical terms?

Two Parables of the Kingdom

Recruit a volunteer to read aloud Matthew 13:31-33. If necessary, tell participants the phrase "kingdom of heaven" is, in Matthew, synonymous with "kingdom of God" in the other Gospels. Discuss:

- What is the surprising contrast at the heart of the first parable? What about in the second parable? *(Note: "Three measures" is a significant amount of flour; "about sixty pounds," according to the NIV.)*
- How are the tree and the flour in these parables images of life?
- How are the mustard seed and the yeast images of God's kingdom?
- Interpreting these parables, Adam writes, "[T]he kingdom of God is not something that comes by divine fiat, instantaneously, simply by God's command," but rather "starts small and comes slowly." Why does God choose to have God's kingdom manifest itself in small and slow ways? When, if ever, have you experienced God's kingdom slowly and on a small scale?

- "[E]ach person who chooses to follow Christ is like the soil in which the mustard seed is planted," writes Adam, "or the dough that is leavened by yeast." Do you agree with this interpretation? Why or why not?
- Adam states that the Kingdom "is not a place, but a way of living" characterized by doing God's will through acts of love. When have small, even slow "acts of kindness, compassion, mercy, goodness, and more" brought about God's kingdom in your life? in the lives of those you know? in your congregation? in society and the world?
- If you were rewriting Jesus's parables using modern imagery, what images for God's kingdom would you choose, and why?

Closing Your Session

Summarize Adam's discussion of the "several senses in which Jesus spoke of the kingdom of God": a present, close-at-hand reality to be experienced here and now; an emerging reality to be prayed and worked for; and a future hope to be fully realized at Jesus's return. On newsprint or markerboard, sketch the diagram in chapter 1 that illustrates Ron Heifetz's explanation of "closing the gap" between the world as it now is and the world as it should be. Read aloud: "[O]ur task, as individual Christians and as churches, is to work to close this gap with the power of the Holy Spirit."

Ask participants to share examples of how they have seen Christians—including, perhaps, themselves—working to "close the gap" between their lives as they are and as God wants them to be, and/or between the world as it is and as God wants it to be. You can offer your own example to spark discussion or summarize the example of The Giving Grove which Adam offers.

Discuss:

- When, if ever, have you experienced God's kingdom as an already present reality?
- How can Christians keep belief in God's kingdom from becoming an obstacle to clearly seeing the world as it is?

- How can Christians cultivate a more faithful imagination for envisioning the world as God wants it to be, even though it is not yet?
- When have you experienced joy in "closing the gap" between the "already" and "not yet" of God's kingdom?
- How does your congregation work to close this gap?
- What is something you will commit to doing before the next session that will help further close this gap?

Closing Prayer

Sovereign God, though you are ruler of all, we confess we have rebelled and still rebel against your rule. Grant us the grace of repentance, that we may offer ourselves, more and more, as those who not only pray for your kingdom to come but also and especially work to do your will, for the sake of and following in the way of Jesus Christ. Amen.

Optional Extensions

- Find one or more hymns or songs in your congregation's hymnal or songbook that use royal imagery for God and/or focus on the kingdom of God. Sing or read the lyrics aloud together as a group. Do any of these hymns or songs quote Jesus? What are their biblical sources or inspirations?

- Invite participants to illustrate Jesus's parables of the mustard seed and the yeast, and/or their own modern parables. Share the illustrations via your congregation's worship bulletin, newsletter, or website.

- Learn more about the work of The Giving Grove, which Adam describes in this chapter (https://www.givinggrove.org/).

SESSION 2

THE WORLD'S MOST IMPORTANT SERMON

Session Goals

This session's reading, reflection, discussion, and prayer will help participants:

- Reflect on the meaning and ethical implications of the "great reversal" reflected in Jesus's Beatitudes (Matthew 5:1-12).
- Identify practical ways they can, as individuals and as congregations, live as "salt" and "light" (Matthew 5:13-16).
- Engage Jesus's challenging interpretations of commandments from the Law (Matthew 5:17-48) to understand more clearly the righteousness to which he calls his followers.
- Consider the Lord's Prayer in the context of Jesus's teaching about private piety (Matthew 6:1-14).
- Examine their attitudes toward wealth and worry in response to Jesus's teachings about money and physical needs (Matthew 6:25-33).
- Articulate criteria they and their congregation use to determine whether what they do is the will of God.

Biblical Foundations

- Matthew 5:1-16
- Matthew 7:21-23

Before Your Session

- Carefully and prayerfully read this session's Biblical Foundations, more than once. Note words and phrases that attract your attention and meditate on them. Write down questions you have and try to answer them, consulting trusted Bible commentaries.
- Carefully read chapter 2 of *The Message of Jesus*, more than once.
- You will need: Bibles for in-person participants and/or screen slides prepared with scripture texts for sharing (identify the translation used); newsprint or a markerboard and markers (for in-person sessions); paper, pens or pencils (in-person).
- If using the DVD or streaming video, preview the session 2 video segment. Choose the best time in your session plan for viewing it.

Starting Your Session

Welcome participants. Discuss:

- What's the most memorable sermon (if any) you've ever heard? What made it so?

Tell participants your group will, in this session, survey much of Jesus's "Sermon on the Mount," found in Matthew 5–7. Point out, as Adam does, that Jesus most likely didn't deliver this material as a single "sermon" on one occasion, but that Matthew compiled teachings Jesus shared "many times in a variety of settings."

Before participants open their Bibles, ask them to brainstorm a list of sayings they may remember from the Sermon on the Mount. Write responses on newsprint or markerboard. If needed, point out this "sermon" contains, among much else, the Beatitudes, the Lord's Prayer, and the Golden Rule.

Discuss:

- Why do you think the Sermon on the Mount has become such a well-known part of Jesus's message, both within and outside of the church?
- Adam says the Sermon on the Mount is an example of "prophetic speech," by which he means speech that is "less foretelling and more forth-telling—speaking hard truths and challenging the status quo." Who do you know or know of whom you would say speaks prophetically in this sense, and why?

Opening Prayer

God Most High and Holy, from the heights of Mount Sinai you instructed your holy people, through Moses, in your law; and on a mountain in Galilee, through your Son Jesus, you instruct all who would follow him in the ways of your reign. As we study the Sermon on the Mount, may you speak again, through your Spirit, teaching how we may walk the paths of righteousness and love that are pleasing to you, life-giving to our neighbors, and for which you created all humanity. Amen.

Watch Session Video

Watch the session 2 video segment together. Discuss:

- Which of Adam's statements most interested, intrigued, surprised, or confused you? Why?
- What questions does this video segment raise for you?

Keep the video in mind as you discuss the book and Bible.

Book Discussion Questions

The Beatitudes

Recruit volunteers to read aloud Matthew 5:2-12, preferably with a different person reading each beatitude (with verses 11-12 counting together as the ninth beatitude). Discuss:

- As Adam points out, these verses are known as "the Beatitudes," from the Latin *beatus*, signifying "happiness, good fortune, or blessedness." Who do you think about when you think about people who are "happy," "fortunate," or "blessed"? Why?
- According to Jesus, who are or will be "the blessed and beautiful" in God's kingdom? What makes Jesus's identification of these people surprising?
- Which of Jesus's Beatitudes resonates most with you, and why? Which one, if any, confuses, challenges, or even worries you most, and why?
- Adam suggests the Beatitudes reflect "the great reversal" of God's kingdom. How so? How do Luke's version of the Beatitudes (6:20-25) and his account of Mary's praise of God (1:46-55) reflect this "great reversal"? How do, or can, those who now have resources, influence, and power find blessing?
- How would your society have to change to treat as blessed those Jesus calls "blessed"? What changes would your congregation need to make? How would you, yourself, need to change?

Living as Salt and Light

Recruit a volunteer to read aloud Matthew 5:13-16. Discuss:

- As Adam explains, the ancient world knew salt as a valuable, life-giving preservative, essential for health and used to enhance flavor. How was salt a good image for God's people then? Is it still a good image? Why or why not?

- What made light a good image for God's people in the ancient world? Is it still a good image? Why or why not?
- What additional images would effectively communicate Jesus's vision of his disciples' mission in today's world?
- The Greek word for "you" in these verses is plural. Why is this distinction significant? Can individuals also live as salt and light? Why or why not?
- What specific "good works" (verse 16)—in Adam's words, "good and beautiful" works—are you and your congregation doing to live as salt and light, and to bring glory to God?

Called to Greater Righteousness

Read aloud Matthew 5:17-20. Explain, as Adam does, that in the Sermon on the Mount, Jesus calls his followers to observe the Law (Torah) with a righteousness greater even than that of Pharisees, who "were highly respected for their apparent faithfulness and devotion to God." In Matthew 5:21-48, Jesus interprets various commandments in ways that make them "infinitely more difficult" to obey.

Form five small groups of participants. Assign each small group one of the following Scriptures:

- Matthew 5:21-26
- Matthew 5:27-32
- Matthew 5:33-37
- Matthew 5:38-42
- Matthew 5:43-48

Instruct each small group to ask these questions about its assigned scripture (you may want to write them on newsprint or markerboard for easy reference):

- What commandment in the Law does Jesus quote? (Many study Bibles, in print and online, will identify the sources of Jesus's quotations; note that no Old Testament text commands hatred of enemies, 5:43.)

- How does Jesus amplify the scope of the quoted commandment?
- Do you think Jesus is using hyperbole (exaggeration) to make his point about this commandment? Why or why not? Does it make you take his words less or more seriously, and why?
- How do or how would you, your congregation, and/or your society be different with serious and consistent obedience to this commandment as Jesus interprets it?

After allowing time for discussion, call small groups back together. Ask volunteers from each group to share insights from their discussion with everyone.

*If you are leading a smaller class and breaking into five small groups isn't feasible, consider choosing one or two of the cited Scriptures to discuss together.

The World's Most Prayed Prayer

Recruit volunteers to read aloud Matthew 6:1-18. If all participants have access to the same translation, read verses 9b-13 in unison. Discuss:

- Jesus discusses three disciplines in this section: giving alms, prayer, and fasting. How comfortable are you with each of these disciplines?
- Why does Jesus command his followers to practice their piety in secret (verses 1-6)? Do his teachings here contradict his teaching about being "light" in 5:16? Why or why not?
- What has your experience been praying the Lord's Prayer (verses 9b-13)?
- Which petition in the Lord's Prayer means the most to you, and why? Which one, if any, confuses or concerns you the most, and why?
- How does Jesus's model prayer, in Adam's words, "shape our hearts and move us to action"? How does it move us "from a me-centered faith to a we-centered faith"?
- What do you think about Jesus's teaching on forgiveness in verse 14?

Money and Worry

Recruit volunteers to read aloud Matthew 6:19-34. Discuss:

- How would you summarize Jesus's attitude toward money?
- "The more freely we give," writes Adam, "the less hold money has on our hearts." Do you agree? Why or why not?
- How much or how little do you or those you know worry about the basic physical needs of food, drink, and clothing Jesus addresses in verses 25-33? Is it possible to worry too little about these needs, as well as too much?
- Adam says Jesus taught his followers that God was able to meet, "not necessarily their wants, but their needs." How do you distinguish between your wants and your needs? How does your congregation? How do you trust God to meet needs?
- What does seeking God's kingdom and righteousness first look like, practically? How, if at all, have you and/or your congregation experienced Jesus's promise in verse 33?

Closing Your Session

Recruit volunteers to read aloud Matthew 7:21-23. Discuss:

- Who does Jesus say will enter the kingdom? Why will those who do not enter be surprised at Jesus's reaction to them?
- Does Jesus's teaching here challenge your understanding of God's grace? Why or why not?
- What criteria do you and your congregation use to determine whether what you are doing is "the will of [the] Father in heaven" (verse 21)? Have you ever determined it was not? What did you do?

Closing Prayer

Lord, in love you confront us and challenge us with your uncompromising call to righteousness—to be perfect as your Father in heaven, and ours, is perfect.

Though we do not claim perfection, we praise you for claiming us as your own and pray your Spirit would continue to strengthen us to more closely pursue the Father's will, that we may be a community shining with your light, glorifying God in your name. Amen.

Optional Extensions

- Sing or read aloud together one or more hymns or songs in your congregation's hymnal or songbook based on material from the Sermon on the Mount; and/or listen to recordings of musical settings of the material. Does this music help you better understand and follow Jesus's teachings? Why or why not?

- Brainstorm "modern Beatitudes" that reflect Jesus's ideas using modern language about who is blessed in today's circumstances. Publish these beatitudes via your congregation's worship bulletin, newsletter, or website.

- Listen to the interview with the Rev. Samuel "Billy" Kyles that Adam mentions: "Rev. Kyles Remembers Martin Luther King, Jr.," NPR Weekend Edition Sunday, January 27, 2010; https://www.npr.org/2010/01/17/122670935/rev–kyles –remembers–martin–luther–king–jr. How, specifically, are you and your congregation "knocking holes in the darkness"?

- As Adam mentions, Luke records a different, shorter version of the Sermon on the Mount, often called the "Sermon on the Plain" (see Luke 6:17). Read Luke 6:20-49. How do you summarize the most notable or significant similarities and differences between these two "sermons"? How does each comfort you? challenge you? Recognizing both are scripture, do you "prefer" one version to the other? Why? Does having two versions of this "sermon" enrich Christian faith and practice? If so, how? If not, why not?

SESSION 3

JESUS SPOKE TO THEM IN PARABLES

Session Goals

This session's reading, reflection, discussion, and prayer will help participants:

- Articulate a working definition of a parable and think about why Jesus favored parables in his teaching.
- Consider how Jesus's parable of the sheep and goats calls his followers today to respond to suffering today.
- Reflect on how Jesus's parable of the good Samaritan still challenges preconceptions about who Jesus's followers are supposed to help and love.
- Ponder how Jesus's parable of the prodigal son offers insights into God's extravagant grace.
- Identify ways they and their congregations can challenge widespread characterizations of Christianity as pushing away people whom Jesus came to seek and save.

Biblical Foundations

- Matthew 25:31-40
- Luke 10:29-37
- Luke 15·11-13, 17-20, 28-32

Before Your Session

- Carefully and prayerfully read this session's Biblical Foundations, more than once. Note words and phrases that attract your attention and meditate on them. Write down questions you have and try to answer them, consulting trusted Bible commentaries.
- Carefully read chapter 3 of *The Message of Jesus*, more than once.
- You will need: Bibles for in-person participants and/or screen slides prepared with scripture texts for sharing (identify the translation used); newsprint or a markerboard and markers (for in-person sessions); paper, pens or pencils (in-person).
- If using the DVD or streaming video, preview the session 3 video segment. Choose the best time in your session plan for viewing it.
- Consider recruiting your readers in advance of your session, as this session's readings are long and would especially benefit from readers' preparing beforehand to read with expression and careful attention to meaning.

Starting Your Session

Welcome participants. Brainstorm with them a list of Jesus's parables. Participants can name aloud parables they remember and/or skim the Gospels for parables. Discuss:

- Adam defines a parable as "a comparison or analogy, aimed at communicating truth, inspiring the heart, or calling people to action." Why did Jesus use parables so much in his teaching?
- Do you have a favorite—or least favorite—parable Jesus told? Why?

- Adam says Jesus's parables sometimes functioned as riddles. How so? When, if ever, has pondering a riddle or puzzle led you to grasp an important truth?
- Where have you encountered parables other than in Jesus's teaching?
- Have you ever used a parable to communicate truth, similar to the way Adam did in his "sermon on manure"? How did people respond to your parable?

Tell participants this session will give your group opportunity to engage with three of Jesus's best-known parables.

Opening Prayer

O God, by grace alone you bring us into the story of your saving work. As we read and reflect on stories your Son Jesus told, may we find again, or for the first time, the places you would have us be in the plot of your liberating love for your people and for the world. May your Spirit excite our imaginations that we, too, may help others see new possibilities for living in your truth, your justice, and your peace. Amen.

Watch Session Video

Watch the session 3 video segment together. Discuss:

- Which of Adam's statements most interested, intrigued, surprised, or confused you? Why?
- What questions does this video segment raise for you?

Keep the video in mind as you discuss the book and Bible below.

Book Discussion Questions

The Sheep and the Goats

Recruit a volunteer to read aloud Matthew 25:31-46. If your group has access to the same translation, everyone can read verses 37-39 and 44 in unison. Discuss:

- What about this parable most interests, excites, confuses, or concerns you, and why?
- Why does Jesus compare the King's future judgment to a shepherd's activity? (Consider also Psalm 23; Ezekiel 34:11-16; John 10:11-18.) What other image(s) might Jesus have used if telling this parable today? Why?
- Why does the King need to separate the "righteous" from the "accursed," and what criteria does he use to do so?
- "Some Christians," writes Adam, "are very uncomfortable with this parable." Why? How comfortable or uncomfortable with it are you?
- Do you think Jesus's parable teaches "the sole criteria for salvation is our works?" Why or why not?
- How does Jesus's parable reflect the "great reversal" that characterizes God's kingdom (as discussed in session 2)?
- How does Jesus's parable "shake us out of resignation and indifference to the suffering of others"?

The Good Samaritan

Recruit volunteers to read aloud Luke 10:25-37, reading as the narrator, the expert in the law, and Jesus. Discuss:

- What about this parable most interests, excites, confuses, or concerns you, and why?
- How is the first question the expert in the law (Torah) asks Jesus a "test" (verse 25)? How does Jesus respond?
- The legal expert presses on because he wants to "vindicate" (NRSVue) or "justify" (ESV) himself, or "prove that he was right" (CEB). When, if ever, have you pressed on in a discussion or argument for the same reason? What happened?
- Skim Leviticus 19. What practical, concrete forms does love for one's fellow Israelite takes in this chapter? How do verses 33-34 command love for non-Israelites?

- Adam writes, "There's something in most of us that wants to know who we don't have to love." Do you agree? Why or why not? When, if ever, have you wondered whether God really meant someone in particular when commanding love of neighbor? What did you do?
- Adam mentions two congregations that found loving their neighbors a challenge: one that appeared to love only its own membership, and another that split in the sixties when the pastor moved to welcome Black people. What particular challenges to loving your neighbors does your congregation face? How are you addressing these challenges?
- What is surprising about who does and doesn't stop to help the wounded man in the story? (See also John 4:9.) How would Jesus produce a similar surprise if he told this parable today?
- How does Jesus's parable transform the question the legal expert asked?
- When have you, like the priest and Levite in Jesus's parable, "passed by on the other side" when confronted with someone who needed help? Why did you do so? When did you stop and help? Why did you do so? How do you determine when you will help and when you will not?

The Prodigal Son

Recruit volunteers to read aloud Luke 15:11-32, reading the roles of the narrator, the father, and the two sons. Discuss:

- What about this parable most interests, excites, confuses, or concerns you, and why?
- Who do you identify with most in this parable, and why?
- How is the younger son "prodigal" (extravagant, wasteful, reckless) in this story? How is the father "prodigal"?
- Is the older son justifiably angry about the homecoming reception his younger brother receives? Why or why not? What do you think about his father's response to his anger?

- Jesus's parable doesn't tell us whether the older brother finally joined the celebration. Do you imagine he did or didn't, and why?
- Luke says Jesus told this parable—and two others about being lost (verses 3-10)—to a crowd composed of "tax collectors and sinners" and religious leaders upset about Jesus's association with them (verses 1-2). How do you imagine people in each of these groups responded to the story, and why?
- Adam finds the father in the story a powerful image of God, the heavenly Father. Do you? Why or why not?
- Has God's mercy toward someone else ever seemed unfair to you? If so, when, and why? If not, why not?

Closing Your Session

Read aloud from *The Message of Jesus*: "Today, Christianity is often more associated with the spirit of the Pharisees [in Luke 15:1-2] and the older brother in Jesus's parable. That spirit pushes away the very people Jesus came to search for and save." Discuss:

- Do you agree with Adam's assessment of how Christianity is usually perceived? Why or why not?
- Can Christians, like Jesus, hold the Sermon on the Mount's high expectations while also offering extravagant grace? If so, how so? If not, why not?
- How does or how could you and your congregation actively seek and welcome the kinds of people Jesus came to seek and save?

Closing Prayer

Loving Jesus, without you, we, too, are lost. We thank you for seeking us, finding us, and restoring us to life. We praise you for your extravagant love, and pray your Spirit would help us extend your love to others—even those we think of as "sinners" and especially those whom you call "the least" in your family. Your grace makes us neighbors to all people. Strengthen us to love them as ourselves, and as you first loved us. Amen.

Optional Extensions

- Distribute newspapers and magazines and invite participants to find photographs they would use to illustrate the parables studied in this session.

- Encourage volunteers to retell or rewrite one or more of the parables studied in this session in modern images and language. Publish the results via your congregation's bulletin, newsletter, and/or website.

- Listen to or read the portion of Rev. Dr. Martin Luther King's "Mountaintop Speech" (April 3, 1968) that Adam discusses in this chapter (about twenty-eight minutes to thirty-four minutes; "Now let me say as I move on to my conclusion…" to "If I do not stop to help the sanitation workers, what will happen to them?"). Check such sites as https://www.youtube .com/ for full audio and https://www.afscme.org/about /history/mlk/mountaintop for full transcript. How does King interpret the parable of the good Samaritan in the context of "dangerous unselfishness"? What "dangerous roads" in your society demand "dangerous unselfishness" from Jesus's followers? How are you and your congregation showing such "dangerous unselfishness"—or how could you?

Session 4

Who Do YOU Say That I Am?

Session Goals

This session's reading, reflection, discussion, and prayer will help participants:

- Identify "I Am" statements as a signature way that John's Gospel speaks of Jesus's identity and significance.
- Understand the Hebrew background of Jesus's "I Am" statements by studying God's revelation of the divine name to Moses in Exodus 3.
- Articulate the meaning of Jesus's seven classic "I Am" images in John's Gospel and ponder their significance for Jesus's followers today.
- Consider the importance of conversations about Jesus.

Biblical Foundations

- John 6:35
- John 8:12

- John 10:7-10
- John 10:11-15
- John 11:21-27
- John 14:5-7
- John 15:1-5

Before Your Session

- Carefully and prayerfully read this session's Biblical Foundations, more than once. Note words and phrases that attract your attention and meditate on them. Write down questions you have and try to answer them, consulting trusted Bible commentaries.
- Carefully read chapter 4 of *The Message of Jesus*, more than once.
- You will need: Bibles for in-person participants and/or screen slides prepared with scripture texts for sharing (identify the translation used); newsprint or a markerboard and markers (for in-person sessions); paper, pens or pencils (in-person).
- If using the DVD or streaming video, preview the session 4 video segment. Choose the best time in your session plan for viewing it.

Starting Your Session

Welcome participants. Invite volunteers to fill in the blank in the following prompt about themselves: "I am _____." (Be ready to fill in the blank for yourself to get discussion going.) Write participants' responses on newsprint or markerboard. Discuss:

- How much, if at all, do your "I am" statements differ from what others would say about you if asked who you are?
- Would you rather tell people, "I am…" or, "I am not…"— and why?

- Does any single one of your "I am" statements communicate the whole truth about who you are?

Read aloud from *The Message of Jesus*: "Among the most interesting, cryptic, yet compelling ways in which Jesus answers the question of his identity and significance in John's Gospel is with two small words, 'I Am.'" Tell participants this session will help your group explore several "I Am" statements of Jesus.

Opening Prayer

God of light and life, in the beginning you spoke all things into being, and in the fullness of time, you spoke your Word made flesh in Jesus Christ. By your Spirit, guide us as we study the words he used to reveal himself to others, that our lives may become living words that reveal his glory and grace. Amen.

Watch Session Video

Watch the session 4 video segment together. Discuss:

- Which of Adam's statements most interested, intrigued, surprised, or confused you? Why?
- What questions does this video segment raise for you?

Keep the video in mind as you discuss the book and Bible.

Book Discussion Questions

I Am, the God of Israel

Recruit volunteers to read aloud Exodus 3:1-15 as the narrator, Moses, and God. Discuss:

- What does this story tell us about who God is?
- Why does Moses ask God for God's name?
- With what words and in what special typeface (if any) does your Bible translate God's name, "YHWH," in verse 14?

- How do you understand the meaning of God's name? How does this story help fill in its meaning?
- Ancient cultures often believed that knowing something or someone's true name conveyed power over that thing or person. How does God's name reject this idea?
- Most English Bible translations substitute "the LORD" for YHWH, just as many observant Jews have, for centuries, substituted "Adonai" ("my Lord") for "YHWH" when reading the Bible in Hebrew aloud. How well do you think the title "Lord" conveys the meaning of God's name, and why?
- Other devout Jews substitute *ha Shem* ("the Name") for "YHWH" when reading the Bible in Hebrew aloud, to show due reverence. Should Christians show similar special reverence for God's name? If so, how? If not, why not?
- What does showing reverence for God's name in everyday life, when not reading scripture aloud, look like?

When I Am Stands Alone

- Several times in John, as Adam notes, Jesus says "I am" (Greek *ego eimi*) by itself, "as a nod to his identification with YHWH." Read these instances of "I am" by itself: 4:25-26; 8:24-28; 13:18-20. What do these exchanges claim about the importance of knowing Jesus as "I am"?
- Read John 18:4-9. How does the physical response of those who've come to arrest Jesus underscore Jesus's identity as "I am"? How does Jesus's control of the situation underscore it?
- Read John 6:16-21(CEB). How do the events of this story support Jesus's self–identification as "I Am"?
- Adam says the story of Jesus calming the storm "is a picture of what Jesus still does in our lives as we trust in him." When, if ever, have you experienced Jesus stilling some kind of "storm" for you? for someone else? for your congregation?

The Classic Seven I Am Statements

As Adam explains, in John's Gospel, Jesus uses seven distinct images to complete the statement "I am..." about himself: "[E]ach statement points to divine attributes that he embodies and divine action that he incarnates."

If your group is large enough, form seven pairs or small groups of participants. Assign each group one of this session's seven Biblical Foundations. (Tell the group studying the Bread of Life image to see also John 6:41 and 6:48; tell the group studying the Light of the World image to see also 9:5).

Instruct each small group to ask these questions about its assigned scripture (you may want to write them on newsprint or markerboard for easy reference):

- What image does Jesus use to complete this statement: "I am..."?
- How is the image appropriate to the occasion or context in which he uses it?
- How is the image related to images for, attributes of, or actions performed by God in the Old Testament? (Consult a concordance or trusted online resources as needed.)
- If Jesus were personally addressing your society today, would he still use this image? If so, why? If not, what equivalent modern image (if any) might he use?
- What does this image say about who Jesus is and his significance for those who have faith in him?
- What ethical implications, if any, does this image have for Jesus's followers today?

After allowing time for discussion, call small groups back together. Ask volunteers from each group to share insights from their discussion with everyone.

If you are leading a smaller group, discuss each of the seven "I Am" images as time allows.

As you see fit, supplement your group's discussion with some or all of these questions:

Bread of Life
- Why do you think Jesus speaks of himself as bread and not some other food?
- How do Deuteronomy 8:3 and Jesus's quotation of it when tempted (Matthew 4:3-4; Luke 4:3-4) inform his use of bread as an image for himself?
- Have you ever been "spiritually malnourished," as Adam describes? What did you do, or what are you doing, about it? How can we avoid such malnourishment?
- How important is the Eucharist (Holy Communion; the Lord's Supper) to your faith? Why? How important is it to your congregation's worship?

Light of the World
- What is the deepest literal, physical darkness in which you have ever found yourself? How did you feel when you came into light—or when light came to you?
- Jesus spoke of himself as light during the festival of Sukkoth (Booths), commemorating the Israelites' wandering the wilderness. How was God light to the people during their wandering (Exodus 13:21)? According to Adam, how was the Temple illuminated during the festival as a reminder of this experience?
- How does Jesus's self-identification as light echo John 1:1-5? What does it mean to you to call Jesus light that darkness has not and cannot overcome?
- How, if ever, have you ever experienced Jesus as light in your emotional, mental, or spiritual darkness?

Gate for the Sheep
- When has a gate been important for your safety and security?
- Why do sheep need protection from wild animals and thieves?

- How does the Bedouin practice Adam describes of shepherds using their own bodies to act as gates for their sheep illuminate what Jesus may mean by using this image for himself?
- Have you experienced Jesus keeping you or those you know safe? If so, how?
- What does the abundant life Jesus says he came to give mean to you?

The Good Shepherd

- What qualities and characteristics distinguish a good shepherd from other shepherds?
- Read Ezekiel 34. What charges does God, through the prophet, make against the leaders or "shepherds" of ancient Israel (34:1-10)? How does God promise to respond (34:11-16)? What does God promise to do among the sheep themselves, and why (34:17-22)? Who does God promise to establish as the new shepherd (34:23-24)? How will the rest of the world reflect God's relationship with God's sheep (34:25-31)?
- When and how do leaders in positions of authority today—in congregations, in communities, in the nations—act as "good shepherds"? Who are the "fat sheep" in today's world from whom "the lean sheep" need protection (Ezekiel 34:20)? How are you and your congregation offering, or how could you offer, such protection?

The Resurrection and the Life

- Why did Jesus wait several days before going to Bethany when he heard Lazarus was ill (John 11:1-6)?
- Why does John emphasize Jesus's love for Lazarus, Mary, and Martha?
- How much, if at all, can you relate to the sisters' disappointment in Jesus (11:21, 32), and why? How does Martha model faith in the midst of disappointment? How would you respond to someone feeling disappointed in or angry with Jesus or God?

- How does Martha initially misunderstand Jesus's promise about Lazarus rising again? Why does she profess faith in Jesus after he identifies himself as "the resurrection and the life" (11:25-27)?
- Why does Jesus, who knows he will bring Lazarus back to life, weep (11:35)? What, if anything, do his tears tell us about grieving, in Adam's words, "as people who have hope" (see also 1 Thessalonians 4:13-14)?
- When, if ever, have you found comfort and hope in Jesus's self-identification as the resurrection and the life?

The Way, the Truth, the Life
- How is Jesus "the way" to God? What makes "the way" synonymous with "the truth" and "the life"?
- How does Jesus's self-identification here serve to reassure and encourage troubled hearts (John 14:1)?
- As Adam notes, some Christians take Jesus's words to mean "all non-Christians will go to hell." What do you think about Adam's interpretation, that any who experience God are experiencing God through Christ, "whether they are conscious of this or not"?
- Should Christians distinguish between Jesus's claims about himself and claims about the Bible, the church, and Christianity? If so, why and how? If not, why not?

The Vine
- What firsthand experience, if any, do you have handling vines, pruning branches, or growing fruit? What insights do these experiences give you into Jesus's image of himself as the vine?
- Read Isaiah 5:1-7. How does this song about Israel as God's vineyard help you understand and appreciate Jesus's image?
- How do you think God "prunes" those who are the branches to Jesus's vine?
- What is the "fruit" Jesus the vine expects his branches to bear?
- How, practically, do Jesus's followers "abide" in him?

Closing Your Session

Adam points out "lengthy dialogues" between Jesus and others are one of the characteristics of John's Gospel. Most of Jesus's "I am" statements occur in these conversations. Discuss:

- What meaning can you find in the fact that Jesus so often reveals who he is during conversation with other people?
- When, if ever, has a conversation with someone else led you to a new or deeper understanding of who Jesus is and what he means for you?
- How does your congregation encourage conversations, within and beyond its membership, about Jesus's identity and significance?
- With whom would you like to have a conversation about Jesus? How might you start such a conversation?

Closing Prayer

Jesus our vine, our sheep gate and good shepherd, bread of life and light of the world: we praise you for all you are and all you give, to us and to the world. Strengthen us, by your Spirit, to follow you, who are the Way; to embrace you, who are the Truth; and to abide in you, who are the Life, that we may love as you love, serve as you serve, and share in your resurrection life, now and forever. Amen.

Optional Extensions

- Research Christian visual art featuring the images Jesus uses in his "I am" statements.

- Sing or read together aloud hymns and songs that use the images in Jesus's "I am" statements.

- Write modern "I am" statements you believe speak to society today. Publish the statements via your congregation's bulletin, newsletter, and/or website.

SESSION 5

FINAL WORDS

Session Goals

This session's reading, reflection, discussion, and prayer will help participants:

- Reflect on the common interest in people's last words (famous and otherwise).
- Consider the original context and continuing significance of the three commands Jesus gave his disciples during the Last Supper.
- Ponder Jesus's "seven last words from the cross," how they communicate different truths about Jesus, and what they mean for believers today.

Biblical Foundations

- John 13:34-35
- Luke 22:24-27
- 1 Corinthians 11:23-26
- John 19:26–30
- Luke 23:33-34a, 39-43, 46
- Mark 15:33-34

Before Your Session

- Carefully and prayerfully read this session's Biblical Foundations, more than once. Note words and phrases that attract your attention and meditate on them. Write down questions you have, and try to answer them, consulting trusted Bible commentaries.
- Carefully read chapter 5 of *The Message of Jesus*, more than once.
- You will need: Bibles for in-person participants and/or screen slides prepared with scripture texts for sharing (identify the translation used); newsprint or a markerboard and markers (for in-person sessions); paper, pens or pencils (in-person).
- If using the DVD or streaming video, preview the session 5 video segment. Choose the best time in your session plan for viewing it.

Starting Your Session

Welcome participants. Discuss:

- Why are people often fascinated by the last words someone speaks?
- What are some "famous last words" you know from historical figures or fictional characters? What makes these words memorable?
- Can you share any memorable last words someone you know personally has spoken? What makes their last words meaningful to you?
- Answer Adam's question: "If you knew you only had days or perhaps hours to live, what would you want to say to your closest friends and family"?

Tell participants that, in this session, your group will explore some of the words Jesus spoke before and during his crucifixion, and what meanings they hold today.

Opening Prayer

O God, your Word made flesh spoke powerful words before his suffering and death. As we read and reflect on the commandments he gave, the prayers he offered, and the promises he gave during the last week of his earthly ministry, may your Spirit move us to faithfully make these words flesh in our daily living. Amen.

Watch Session Video

Watch the session 5 video segment together. Discuss:

- Which of Adam's statements most interested, intrigued, surprised, or confused you? Why?
- What questions does this video segment raise for you?

Keep the video in mind as you discuss the book and Bible below.

Book Discussion Questions

Three Commandments at the Last Supper

Read aloud from *The Message of Jesus*: "At the Last Supper, Jesus gave three commands or mandates to his disciples, and to us: Love one another, serve one another, and remember me."

Form three small groups of participants. Assign each group one of the following scriptures to read and discuss:

- "Love one another" (John 13:12-15, 34-35)
- "Serve one another" (Luke 22:24-30)
- "Remember me" (1 Corinthians 11:23-26)

Each group should consider these questions in their discussion (you may want to write them on newsprint or markerboard for ease of reference):

- What prompts Jesus to give the command he gives?
- What's "at stake"—what practical difference does obeying this command make?

- How do you and your congregation obey this command today?

After allowing sufficient time for discussion, reconvene the whole group. Invite a volunteer from each small group to report on highlights of their discussion. As needed, use the questions below to prompt discussion.

Love One Another
- How is Jesus washing his disciples' feet a demonstration of his love for them?
- Does your congregation literally follow Jesus's example of foot washing? Why or why not? What other specific actions, if any, might convey love today in the way Jesus's washing of his disciples' feet did then?
- What is "new" about Jesus's commandment to love each other?
- Adam says love, as Jesus defines love, "is not a feeling, but a way of living and being." How so? Does this definition make Jesus's command easier or more difficult to obey—or does it make no difference? Why?
- "Sadly today," Adam writes, "Christianity is often associated with everything but love." Do you agree with his assessment? Why or why not?
- Christianity isn't the only religion to teach love. What, if anything, sets Christian love apart?

Serve One Another
- What appears to spark the disciples' argument about greatness (Luke 22:22-27)?
- How will lives of service set Jesus's followers apart from the "kings of the Gentiles"?
- How did Jesus serve others during his earthly ministry? According to Mark 10:43-45, what was Jesus's greatest act of service?

Remember Me

- Read or skim 1 Corinthians 11. Why is Paul reminding his readers in Corinth of what he taught them about the Lord's Supper?

- Do Jesus's words that Paul records differ in any way from the words used in your congregation's Communion celebrations? If so, how? Do you think these differences are significant? Why or why not?

- How had the Corinthians forgotten Jesus? How do Christians today, even those who invoke Jesus's name, forget Jesus?

- Have you or your congregation ever forgotten Jesus? How did you, or how will you, remember him?

- Is thankfully remembering Jesus part of your regular meals? Why or why not?

The Seven Last Words from the Cross

Read aloud from *The Message of Jesus*: "Though Jesus hung on the cross for six hours, we have only seven statements from those hours of agony. If it inflicted pain for Jesus to speak, then every word must be counted as important."

Point out, as Adam does, that the traditional "seven last words" Jesus spoke on his cross are collected from the four Gospels; no one Gospel contains them all and, except in one instance, no Gospel repeats statements found in another.

Ask: "Why do you think the different Gospels contain different words from Jesus as he died?"

Form three small groups of participants (ideally, put participants in different groups than they were in previously). Assign each group one of the following Scriptures to read and discuss:

- Mark 15:33-37 and Matthew 27:45-50
- Luke 23:32-34, 39-46
- John 19:26-30

Each group should consider these questions in their discussion (you may want to write them on newsprint or markerboard for ease of reference):

- Which of the "last words from the cross" does this scripture record?
- What prompts Jesus to speak the word(s) he does?
- What do you learn about Jesus from the "last words" in this scripture?
- What meaning do you find in these words today?

After allowing sufficient time for discussion, reconvene the whole group. Invite a volunteer from each small group to report on highlights of their discussion. As needed, use the questions below to prompt discussion.

Questions for Mark/Matthew Group
- "Jesus appears to be saying that God had abandoned him," writes Adam. Do you think God abandoned Jesus at his crucifixion? Why or why not?
- How do the bystanders misunderstand Jesus's words? How do they respond? When, if ever, have you witnessed people misunderstanding the cry of someone in pain? What, if anything, did you do about it?
- Read Psalm 22. Why did King David feel abandoned by God? How does he feel by the psalm's end, and why? Why did Jesus choose to quote this psalm?
- Adam says, "The very act of crying out this prayer is an act of faith." How so?
- Have you ever felt abandoned by God? When? What happened? What would you say to or do for someone who felt abandoned by God?

Questions for Luke Group
- Adam notes the Greek word for *forgive* literally means "to release or let go." What is Jesus praying God will "let go" in verse 34? What is he letting go in making this prayer?

- Do you think Jesus wanted bystanders to hear his prayer? Why or why not?
- How does Adam suggest Jesus's prayer is a prayer "not only for those standing at the cross, but for all of humanity"? What do you think about this suggestion?
- How easy or difficult do you find it to pray that God will forgive someone else? How easy or difficult do you find it to forgive someone yourself? How are the two actions related?
- How do you account for the two criminals' different reactions to Jesus in verses 39-41?
- What does the second criminal's request of Jesus in verse 42 mean? What does Jesus's answer to him mean?
- How is the second criminal a model for those who pray to Jesus today?
- Adam notes that, in verse 46, Jesus quotes Psalm 31. Read Psalm 31. How is David's expression of faith in the psalm also appropriate to Jesus's crucifixion?
- Following William Barclay's lead, Adam imagines Jesus is praying a childhood prayer as he commends his spirit to God. Which childhood prayers, if any, do you still pray, and why? How often do you pray the Scriptures, as Jesus did?
- When, if ever, have you prayed Jesus's prayer of trust in God as your own? What happened?

Questions for John Group

- How does Jesus demonstrate his concern for his mother? What implications do his words have for how his disciples should care for their parents? What implications, if any, do they hold for other family relationships?
- How do Jesus's words about his mother and closest disciple create a new kind of family relationship? How is your congregation living out this relationship?

- Adam suggests Jesus's statement that he is thirsty carries a deeper meaning. How do John 4:7-14 and John 7:37-39 help illuminate this deeper meaning?
- Why does Adam suggest Jesus's word in verse 30 is not a "cry of defeat" but a "shout of victory"? What do you think?

Closing Your Session

Ask:

- Which of Jesus's "last words" that we studied and discussed in this session mean the most to you today, and why?
- Which of his "last words" would you most like to offer to someone else, and why? How have or how might you do so?

Closing Prayer

Lord Jesus, for all the words you spoke before your death, because you have been raised and because you rule in power, you have not yet spoken your "last words," but are speaking still. By your Spirit, when we speak, may we echo your words of grace and peace, that all may hear and welcome your message of love and life. Amen.

Optional Extensions

- Study one or more of the other occasions in the last week of Jesus's earthly ministry in which he gave some "last words": his entry into Jerusalem, his actions in the temple, his "little apocalypse" on the Mount of Olives, his prayer before his arrest, and his trials.

- Adam points to Oskar Schindler as "a dramatic picture of what it means to love and serve others." Watch the scenes from Schindler's List (1993) in which Itzhak Stern (Ben Kingsley) types the list of factory workers Schindler (Liam Neeson) is saving (from about 2 hours, 19 minutes, when

Schindler makes his proposal to a Nazi, to about 2 hours, 25 minutes, when Stern says, "The list is life"), and/or the scene in which Schindler says he could have saved more people (from about 2 hours, 56 minutes as Schindler and the people are leaving the camp, to about 3 hours, 1 minutes, as Schindler's car drives away). What other dramatic examples of love and service from history can you think of? How can paying attention to such examples be helpful or unhelpful?

SESSION 6

THE RESURRECTION AND THE LIFE

Session Goals

This session's reading, reflection, discussion, and prayer will help participants:

- Reflect on popular and personal images of and beliefs about heaven.
- Consider how Jesus's teaching in Matthew 22 about marriage not existing in the resurrection speaks to our deep friendships and nonsexual love relationships in this life.
- Explore what Jesus's parable of the rich man and Lazarus has to say about justice in this life and in the next.
- Think about why Jesus uses "my Father's house" in John 14 as an image for heaven.
- Wonder together about the continuing significance of some questions Jesus asked his followers after his resurrection.
- Identify specific ways in which they will respond to the message of Jesus by living as his witnesses.

Biblical Foundations

- Matthew 22:29-33
- Luke 16:19-31
- John 14:1-3
- Matthew 28:16-20

Before Your Session

- Carefully and prayerfully read this session's Biblical Foundations, more than once. Note words and phrases that attract your attention and meditate on them. Write down questions you have, and try to answer them, consulting trusted Bible commentaries.
- Carefully read chapter 6 of *The Message of Jesus*, more than once.
- You will need: Bibles for in-person participants and/or screen slides prepared with Scripture texts for sharing (identify the translation used); newsprint or a markerboard and markers (for in-person sessions); paper, pens or pencils (in-person).
- If using the DVD or streaming video, preview the session 6 video segment. Choose the best time in your session plan for viewing it.

Starting Your Session

Welcome participants. Discuss:

- When you think about heaven, what's the first thing that comes to your mind?
- What did you think about heaven when you were a child? Do you think differently about heaven now? Why or why not?
- What images of heaven are most prevalent in culture? What do you think or feel about these images?
- Do you have a favorite Bible verse about heaven? If so, what is it, and why?
- What do you think most people don't understand about heaven?

- Adam writes, "To listen to some Christians, you might think that the primary focus of Jesus's entire message and ministry was about heaven and how to get there." Do you agree with his assessment? Why or why not?
- How "primary" of a focus is heaven in your faith? in your congregation?

Tell participants that, in this final session together, your group will explore some of what Jesus said about heaven and the afterlife, and what they can mean for Christians today.

Opening Prayer

Living God, in the resurrection of Jesus Christ you have given your people new birth into a living hope. May this hope, by the Spirit's power, encourage us as we study the Scriptures, giving us confidence that in Jesus's words about the Resurrection life and heaven, we may hear what you want us to know and believe about the future you have prepared and which, through him, we may experience even now. Amen.

Watch Session Video

Watch the session 6 video segment together. Discuss:

- Which of Adam's statements most interested, intrigued, surprised, or confused you? Why?
- What questions does this video segment raise for you?

Keep the video in mind as you discuss the book and Bible below.

Book Discussion Questions

Marriage in Heaven?

Recruit one volunteer to read aloud Matthew 22:23-28, followed by another volunteer reading aloud 22:29-33. Discuss:

- Why do these Sadducees ask Jesus a question about a future resurrection in which they don't believe?
- How could answering this question have gone badly for Jesus, and how does he avoid a negative outcome with his actual answer?
- Jesus accuses his questioners of knowing "neither the scriptures nor the power of God." Is it possible to know one of these without the other? How so?
- How do you understand Jesus's teaching that marriage won't exist in the Resurrection? How do you react to it?
- What do you think of Adam's interpretation "that our romantic affections and our sex drives will give way to deep friendships" and nonsexual love? How might this idea shape the way we value such friendships and love in our lives now?
- What does Jesus's teaching have to say to people who are not married in this life?
- How does Jesus use God's self-identification as the God of Abraham, Isaac, and Jacob (Exodus 3:6) as support for his belief in the Resurrection? What does thinking about God as "God of the living" make you think or feel?

The Rich Man and Lazarus

Recruit volunteers to read aloud Luke 16:19-31, taking the roles of the narrator (Jesus), the rich man, and Father Abraham. Discuss:

- As Adam states, "The point of the parable is not to give a theology of heaven and hell, or even a theology of salvation." What would you say is the parable's point?
- Adam notes the parable reflects an image of the afterlife common in first-century Jewish and Greek thought. What are the major features of this image, judging from the parable?
- Why does Father Abraham say Lazarus is receiving comfort and "good things" in the afterlife (verse 25)? What is Father Abraham's attitude toward the rich man?

- How is the rich man's attitude toward Lazarus in the afterlife like or unlike his attitude toward Lazarus during his earthly life?
- Do you think Lazarus is aware of the rich man in the afterlife? Why or why not?
- Why does Father Abraham discount the ability of someone who has been raised from death to move the rich man's brothers to repentance?
- How important to you personally is the idea that, in the afterlife, wrongs you experienced will be redressed? How important is it to others you know or know of? Why?
- How has the hope of justice in the afterlife been important to Christians throughout history?
- Jesus's parable is fictional. How much reality about the afterlife do you think it presents? Why?
- How much or how little does the idea of torment after death for wrongdoing motivate you to do what is right, and why?

"I Go to Prepare a Place for You"

Recruit a volunteer to read aloud John 14:1-3. Discuss:

- Why are Jesus's disciples "troubled" at the time he speaks these words? What reason(s) does Jesus give them to not be troubled?
- Jesus appeals to his disciples' trust in his truthfulness (verse 2). Who is someone, other than Jesus, whom you trust will always tell you the truth?
- Adam notes, "The Greek word for house is *oikia* and it also can mean household or family—the people who live in a house." To what is Jesus referring when he talks about his "Father's house"? How do you respond to this image, and why?
- How does Jesus prepare a place in his Father's house or family for his followers?
- "My Father's house has room to spare" (verse 2, CEB). What ethical implications for this life, if any, does the ample room in God's household have for those who claim belonging in that household?

- "I am reminded," writes Adam, "that this world is not our home." How ought Christians to live in a world that is not their home? To what extent, if any, should and can Christians make this world like the "place of beauty and joy" that is our "home" in Christ?
- Where and when do you most feel "at home" in this life? What clues about what heaven will be like, if any, do you think you can glean from that experience?

Jesus's Easter Questions

Recruit four volunteers to read aloud Luke 24:13-32, taking the roles of the narrator, Cleopas, and the other disciple (two volunteers can alternate reading verses 19b-24, or even read them in unison), and Jesus. Discuss:

- What keeps Cleopas and the other disciple from recognizing Jesus when he walks with them on the road?
- Why does Jesus initiate conversation with these two disciples— and why does he do so with questions (verses 17, 19)?
- How does Jesus's question in verse 26 differ from his questions earlier in this conversation?
- Why are the disciples finally able to recognize Jesus (verses 30-31)? To what extent, if any, do you think Jesus's questions prepared them to recognize him?
- How does the disciples' question to each other in verse 32 differ from all earlier questions in this conversation?
- When, if ever, have you asked someone else whether they have experienced Jesus's presence?

Recruit three volunteers to read aloud John 21:15-17, taking the roles of the narrator, Simon Peter, and Jesus. Discuss:

- Answer Adam's question: "Why does John record this embarrassing story about Peter, and the excruciating recital of these questions three times?"

- Would you say, as Adam says about himself, that you have ever denied Jesus? Why or why not? If so, do you believe Jesus has restored you to fellowship with him, as he restored Peter? Why or why not?
- Who are Jesus's "lambs" and "sheep," and what does it look like for you and you congregation to "tend" and "feed" them today?

Closing Your Session

Recruit a volunteer to read aloud Matthew 28:16-20. Read aloud from *The Message of Jesus*: "Jesus calls his disciples to be his witnesses, and that ultimately involves not merely telling others but also living the message he taught them.... Having studied the message of Jesus, how will you respond to it?" Invite volunteers to talk briefly about their response to Adam's question.

Thank participants for sharing this study of *The Message of Jesus* with you. Ask volunteers to talk about what insights they will remember most and/or what questions the study leaves them with, and how they will seek answers to those questions.

Closing Prayer

Jesus our risen Lord, you still charge those who follow you to proclaim your gospel in word and deed. May your Spirit always fill, guide, and lead us, making us ever more faithful witnesses to you, embodying your message of God's might, mercy, and saving love. May the study we have completed continue to bear fruit that is pleasing in your sight, and may we never stop learning how to live as your disciples. Amen.

Optional Extension

- Close your session by singing or reading aloud together one of your group's favorite Easter hymns or songs.

Watch videos based on *The Message of Jesus* with Adam Hamilton through Amplify Media.

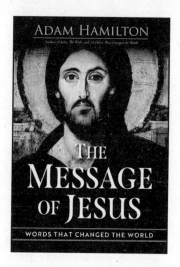

Amplify Media is a multimedia platform that delivers high quality, searchable content with an emphasis on Wesleyan perspectives for churchwide, group, or individual use on any device at any time. In a world of sometimes overwhelming choices, Amplify gives church leaders and congregants media capabilities that are contemporary, relevant, effective and, most importantly, affordable and sustainable.

With *Amplify Media* church leaders can:

- Provide a reliable source of Christian content through a Wesleyan lens for teaching, training, and inspiration in a customizable library
- Deliver their own preaching and worship content in a way the congregation knows and appreciates
- Build the church's capacity to innovate with engaging content and accessible technology
- Equip the congregation to better understand the Bible and its application
- Deepen discipleship beyond the church walls

Ask your group leader or pastor about Amplify Media and sign up today at www.AmplifyMedia.com.